COFFEE AND A PRAYER

90 Peaceful Prayers

Andrea Lende

This book is dedicated to my father, Rev. Dr. Richard Einerson, who has given 60 years to ministry and has written his own prayer book, Prayers of the People, Pastoral Prayers for Worship and Personal Devotion.

CONTENTS

INTRODUCTION

I started writing prayers to the Lord a number of years ago after reading Psalm 5:3 where King David writes, "In the morning You hear my voice, O Lord; in the morning I prepare [a prayer a sacrifice] for You and watch and wait [for You to speak to my heart]." God is so faithful. As I wrote prayers to Him, He answered back.

I have shared these prayers with others who found great peace in reading them. They also found hope during a hopeless time.

I encourage you to read the first prayer today because there is no better time than right now to be covered in His peace and lifted up in hope.

HE WILL NOT ALLOW ME TO SLIP

O Lord, my God, thank You for watching over me and taking care of me continually, without missing a moment of the day. Thank You for Your protection. Thank You for Your provision. Thank You for teaching me and ministering to my spirit. May You cover me in peace today. May You strengthen every fiber of my being as I move toward Your will for my life. Your Word says that You will keep me from slipping. I believe in You, Father, and I believe in Your Word. May it be so. May I worship at Your feet. I praise You, Lord. I praise Your Name! You are greatly to be praised. You have made me for Your purpose. May Your will be done. Bend my will to Yours. May Your desires be my desires, Father. Keep my eyes on You today. Help me bless someone this day. Thank You for hearing my prayer.

Answer: I AM with you, My child, and will keep you from slipping.

Response: Thank You, Almighty God and Father.

SEARCH FOR PEACE

O Lord, my God, thank You for showing me the value of peace. Thank You for continuing to remind me that Your peace and Your presence are all I need. You have been so gracious to me. You continue to wrap me up in a blanket of peace as the world around me feeds on chaos. You continue to shower me with Your mercy. You show me how much You love me no matter how short I come to perfection. Though I miss the mark, You love me anyway. I am never out of Your care. I cannot run from You, Lord. Thank You for never letting go of me. Thank You for choosing me to know You. Help me stay in Your peace today as the cares of this world compass about me. Help me look to You and not the world, Father. Keep my eyes on You. Help me bless someone today. Thank You for hearing my prayer.

Answer: My peace is upon you, My child.

Response: Thank You, most gracious and loving God.

LOVE COVERS ALL

O Lord, my God, thank You for Your continued outpouring of Wisdom into my heart and soul. Thank You for showing me over and over again that love covers all. I desire peace and simplicity and know that being led by love will provide an opening to both. Help me turn the busyness of this life into purpose. Help me give up things that cloud and muddy up my life. Please help me live with clarity and love those around me with Your boundless love. Help me see others as You see them. Put Your compassion in my heart so I can bend to their needs instead of seeking to gratify my own desires. Help me know You are taking care of everything I need and want. Thank You for working in every circumstance of my life. Thank You for watching over me and protecting me and the family You have given me. I can ask for nothing more. Help me bless someone this day. Thank You for hearing my prayer.

Answer: I AM love and will put My love in your heart so you can do My will.

Response: Strengthen me to do all You have for me to do.

CAST YOUR CARES
ON HIM

O Lord, my God, thank You for all You do for me and all You are. Thank You for working in every circumstance of my life. Thank You for allowing me to give you my fears, anxieties, cares, failures, and mishaps. Thank You for caring enough about me to want to take all these worries from me. Thank You for righting my wrongs, and for working out everything for my good. Your constant care of me is perfect. I ask You to calm the raging storm around me and help me know You have a perfect plan for me and the family You have given me. Keep my eyes on You as the world seems to spin out of control. Help me look to the heavens instead of the chaos that whirls around me. May Your perfect peace rest on me this day. May I sit in Your presence and be made whole in this moment. Thank You, Father, for all You do for me and all You are. Undeserving of Your love and attention, I cannot escape it. Help me bless someone this day. Thank You for hearing my prayer.

Answer: I AM with you, My child, and have a plan for you even as these days look uncertain. Keep your eyes on Me.

Response: Help me look to You for all that I need and desire, Father.

THE LORD IS MY SHEPHERD

O Lord, my God, thank You for all You do for me and all that You are. Thank You for Your constant presence in my life. Thank You for watching over me and the family You have given me. Forgive me for going my own way. Forgive me for not letting You lead and guide me as You desire. Help me allow You to lead me, Lord. Help me be humble and allow You to take me where You want me to go. Help me allow You to Shepherd me and bring me to the best pastures and most peaceful places. Only You truly know my needs and how to meet them. Help me follow You and heed Your voice. Help me hear Your whispers and be obedient to Your directions. Keep me at Your feet, Lord. Keep me seeking You above all else. Calm my fears and quiet my anxious mind. Replace all of that with Your perfect peace. Help me serve others with a joyful heart today. Help me bless someone this day. Thank You for hearing my prayer.

Answer: I AM with you to lead you into all the wonderful places I have for you and keep you safe, My child.

Response: May I be obedient to Your leading, most gracious and mighty God.

I AM WITH YOU

O Lord, my God, thank You for all You do for me and all You are. Thank You that You sent Your Son to live and die for me so I may be covered by His blood. Thank You that He is beside me today as He said He would be. I do not deserve Your or His presence in my life but You offer it freely, without reserve, and wait for me to call upon You for all I need. As this day begins, I give You all my anxious thoughts and fears and ask You to cover me with Your peace. I love You, Father, and pray You keep me focused on You instead of the uncertainty surrounding me. Help me sit at Your feet and soak up Your love, grace, and mercy until it overflows in my heart. Then let me offer help to someone in need. Help me be Your hands and Your heart to someone this day. Show me who needs You, Lord. Help me love with Your love. Help me serve with compassion and be strong enough to allow You to work through me. Strengthen me in every way, Lord. Help me bless someone today. Thank You for hearing my prayer.

Answer: I AM with you, My child, and My peace is upon you as I strengthen you so you may help those in need.

Response: Thank You, most gracious and loving Father.

ONE THING I ASK FOR

O Lord, my God, thank You for spending time with me. Thank You for always being ready to fill my heart and soul. May Your presence be upon me and Your grace carry me this day. Thank You for showing me the beauty of You and Your love. Thank You for loving me beyond my comprehension. Help me receive Your love today, Father. Help me bask in Your presence. Don't let the cares of this world cloud or dampen my ability to sit with You and receive all that You have to give me. Just as a child receives wonderful gifts from their parents, help me receive from You. I ask You strengthen me to meet the challenges of this day. Ready me for Your service, Lord. Help me help others and serve with joy. Don't let me miss anyone who needs Your tender care. Thank You for being my Rock and my Strength. May Your perfect will be done, Lord. Guide my every step, thought, and deed as I walk through this day. May Your protection be upon me, the family You have given me, and all the families in this blessed nation and around the world. May we all look to You and be caught up in Your presence today. Help me bless someone this day. Thank You for hearing my prayer.

Answer: I AM watching over you and all people and desire to spend time with you, My child.

Response: Thank You, Almighty God and Father.

BE CAREFUL WHAT
YOU HEAR

O Lord, my God, thank You for Your perfect Word in due season. You never disappoint. You always show me exactly what I need to see at exactly the moment I need to see it. You are my Rock. You are my Strength. You are my everything that I need today and every day. May You fill my heart with joy. May You fill my soul with peace. Help me meditate on You all day long. Replace my fear with Your wisdom, Lord, and help me know all is according to Your plan. Keep my thoughts on You, Father. Keep my eyes on You. Drown out the noise of this world, and help me praise You, Lord. You are great and greatly to be praised! You, and only You, are Creator and Designer of this universe. May Your will be done. Lead and guide me, Lord. Quiet my mind and lead me to the still and restful waters. Help me bless someone this day. Thank You for hearing my prayer.

Answer: I AM with you, My child, to watch over and protect you – simply follow Me.

Response: Keep me seeking You and help me follow You, Lord.

HIS ANGELS WATCH OVER YOU

O Lord, my God, thank You for taking care of me and the family You have given me. Thank You for watching over us and protecting us. Thank You for sending Your angels to watch over us in a very special way. You assure me no evil will take over and consume me for You are caring for me. Lord, I pray You strengthen my faith. Help me believe in all that You are in a more profound way today than yesterday. Replace my fears and anxious thoughts with peace. Lift me up to You when I start sinking in my own mind. Keep my thoughts on You throughout this day, Lord. May Your presence surround me and lift me to praise Your Name. You are Almighty God, Creator of the universe, and Maker of my heart. Help me love You with all my heart, Lord. Help me serve You today and every day. How I long to be sitting at Your feet. How I long to worship You in heaven. Help me do all You have for me to do here, Father, and bring me home to You. Keep my eyes on You today. Help me bless someone this day. Thank You for hearing my prayer.

Answer: I AM watching over you and your family and will deliver you from all harm.

Response: Thank You, most gracious God and Father.

KEEP BELIEVING

O Lord, my God, thank You for Your Word. Thank You for continually bringing me to the scripture I need for each day. Thank You for ministering to me and meeting my every need. Help me recount Your blessings day and night. Help me remember the works of Your hand in my life so my faith is strengthened. You, Lord, have faithfully provided for me and the family You have given me. You have watched over us and protected us. You have blessed us when no blessing seemed possible. You have healed us from every disease. And Your Word says that You will keep us from harm. I stand on Your Word today, Lord. I believe in Your Word. May You strengthen my faith even more, Father, so I do not waver throughout today. I praise You, Lord! Help me praise You until the sun sets this evening and wake up praising You as the sun comes up in the morning. Keep my thoughts on Your wonderful works, all You have done, and all the promises You have made to me. Help me do all You have for me to do here, Lord. Ready me for Your service. Help me love all those You put in front of me. Help me bless someone this day. Thank You for hearing my prayer.

Answer: Keep believing and do not give into fear for I will take care of you.

Response: Thank You, most gracious and wonderful God.

THERE IS NO FEAR IN LOVE

O Lord, my God, thank you for showing me that love is far more powerful than fear. Thank You for leading me as I read Your Word. Thank You for gently compassing me back into love. May You fill my heart and soul with Your love so I can be a vessel for You instead of a vessel that spreads fear. Help me love those who are close to me today and serve them with joy. May joy flood my heart! Help me be thankful for all You do for me. May my heart be grateful for all I have. As I recount all of Your blessings my heart is filled with gratitude. May Your peace surround me today. Thank You for sending Your Son to teach me and give His life for me so that I can come to You and sit in Your presence. One moment in Your presence is far greater than a lifetime without it. Help me bless someone this day. Thank You for hearing my prayer.

Answer: I AM with you and My Holy Spirit is inside of you so that My love is made perfect in you.

Response: Undeserving of Your love and grace, thank You, most gracious and merciful God and Father.

SWEET COMMUNION WITH GOD

O Lord, my God, thank You for Your Word. Thank You for the wisdom in Your Word. Thank You for the people You use to bring new revelation to my spirit. Thank You for King David. My spirit is uplifted, once again, as I read His songs to You. Thank You for being as available to me as You were to David, a great king, warrior, and servant of Yours. Thank You for waiting upon me until I come to You and give you my heart. Thank You for gently showing me Your love and changing the direction of my desires toward You. Thank You for the peace You cover me in. Thank You for Your perfect will. Help me continue to seek after You, Lord. Keep me at Your feet. Keep me longing to know more of You and Your ways. Show me more, Father, and grant me wisdom. Help my heart and mind be led by Your truth. Lead and guide my every step. Help me bless someone this day. Thank You for hearing my prayer.

Answer: I take pleasure in spending time with you, My child, and will continue leading you closer to Me.

Response: Undeserving of Your love and attention, thank You, most gracious God and Father.

ALL THINGS ARE POSSIBLE

O Lord, my God, thank You for showing me I need You. Thank You for showing me I need to be continually strengthened by You. Help my weakness of faith, Lord, as difficulties arise. Calm my fears and quiet the chaos around me. Help me know You are working out every circumstance perfectly. Help me know Your plan is being executed and Your will is done, always. Keep me at Your feet today, Lord. May Your peace be upon me as I walk through this day. Lead and guide my every step. I look to You, Father, for direction, strength, peace, grace, and a quiet place to rest in You. Thank You for all You do and all You are. Help me bless someone this day. Thank You for hearing my prayer.

Answer: I AM with you, My child, and will you lead into all peace and rest in My presence.
Response: Thank You, Almighty God and Father.

HE DELIVERS YOU

O Lord, my God, thank You for sending Your angel to watch over me, set up camp around me, and protect me. Thank You for showing me the perfect scripture today that assures me of Your protection and deliverance. Thank You for bringing me close to You, Father. Thank You for lifting me up out of the mire and directing me toward You and Your love. Thank You for loving me so perfectly. As the world disappoints, You will never disappoint. You will always make a way for me to be loved and cared for by You. Increase my faith, Lord. As the world spins out of control, bring me to a place of complete faith. Keep me at Your feet seeking You as the chaos ensues. Drown the noise of this world out and help me hear Your every whisper. Give me the strength to obey You and You, alone. May I rest at Your feet, Lord. Fill me with Your Holy Spirit as I spend time in Your presence so I may serve as You desire. Help me do all You have for me to do. Help me bless someone this day. Thank You for hearing my prayer.

Answer: I AM watching over you, protecting you, and filling you with My Spirit.

Response: Thank You, Almighty God and Father.

WITH YOUR WHOLE HEART

O Lord, my God, thank You for showing me wisdom through Your Word today. Thank You for showing me that loving You is the most powerful act I can do today and every day. Help me praise You all day long even when I feel weak. You are Almighty God and greatly to be praised! Fill my heart, soul, and mind with blessed thoughts of You all day long, Father. You have blessed me beyond measure with Your holy presence, and I pray You will continue to flood my heart with Your Holy Spirit. Keep my eyes on You, Lord. Keep me in Your presence. Bring my mind and thoughts to You constantly throughout this day. Help me focus more on You and less on the world and all of its troubles. May Your will be done over mine, Lord. Ready me for Your service. Help me serve with joy, Father. Keep me seeking You and all You desire me to know. I pray for more wisdom – as much as You will give me. May You lead and guide my every step, thought, and word today, Lord. Fill my spirit with love for You as I walk through this day. Help me bless some-one today. Thank You for hearing my prayer.

Answer: I AM with you and grant you increasing wisdom as I fill you with My Holy Spirit.

Response: Thank You, most gracious, loving, and powerful God.

HE KEEPS YOU FROM FALLING

O Lord, my God, thank You for reminding me You are All Powerful and Almighty. Thank You for reminding me You are my Keeper. You keep me from stumbling, slipping, and falling. You keep me close to You. Thank You for providing a way for me to come to You blameless and faultless. Thank You for sending Your Son to die for me so I can be completely Yours and be seen by You as perfect. Fill my soul and spirit today with Your love, Father, so I may praise You! You are more deserving of all the praise I can give. You save me every day, Lord. Every day You show me more of You and save me one more time. Thank You, Lord, for showing me more of You and Your Son every time I open Your Word. Thank You that I can freely read Your Word and be blessed. Thank You that I can freely praise and worship You. Thank You that I can share Your Word with those You call upon as Yours. I ask You keep me in all ways, Lord. Keep me Yours. Continue to keep me from stumbling, slipping, and falling. Keep me at Your feet. Help me bless someone this day. Thank You for hearing my prayer.

Answer: I will keep you, My child, and will keep all of My children as My own.

Response: Undeserving of Your love, attention, and safety, Lord, thank You.

EVEN IN OUR WEAKNESS

O Lord, my God, thank You for reminding me You have written a beautiful story of my life. You already know my faults and weaknesses and love me through them. Your plans for me are lovely, and I need only to step into Your will to experience Your goodness. Help me sit in Your presence this morning, Father. Help me be restored and refreshed by You this day. Fill me with Your love and Your Holy Spirit so I may be used by You, Lord. Thank You for showing me that my imperfections cannot keep me from Your glorious plan. Help me be obedient to You in every way, Father. Help me hear every whisper and follow You. May You lead and guide my every step today. Set a guard upon my mouth so I only speak life to those around me. Help me build up their spirits and minds and not tear down. May Your peace be upon me and this household, Father. Keep us looking to You and seeking Your will. May we bend to You in every way. Thank You for watching over us and protecting us, Lord. Put Your compassion in our hearts so we may serve You. Help me bless someone this day. Thank You for hearing my prayer.

Answer: I AM with you and your household this day and every day, and am watching over and protecting you, My child.

Response: Thank You most glorious and gracious God.

HE WILL GIVE YOU THE DESIRES OF YOUR HEART

O Lord, my God, thank You for all You do for me and all You are. I bask in Your greatness today, Father. I delight myself in You. You are great and wonderful – too wonderful for me to even understand. May I always take wonder in You and delight in You, Lord. As I watch You work, I become more awestruck by Your majesty. You truly are a God of miracles here and now. You are still showing Yourself magnificent, Father. Help me not miss You and what You do. Help me see every good thing that You do. Continue to change my heart and bend my will to Yours. Help me do everything You have for me to do, Lord. Strengthen me in every way and keep me seeking Your will over mine. Thank You for watching over and protecting me and the family You have given me. May Your peace and mercy continue to be upon us. Help me bless someone this day, Lord. Thank You for hearing my prayer.

Answer: I AM the Great I AM and will lead you to Me and My will.

Response: You are great and greatly to be praised, Father!

A HEAVENLY KNIGHTHOOD

O Lord, my God, thank You for showing me Your Might and Strength! Thank You for showing me You have an army of angels ready to do Your work and praise Your Name. I praise You, Lord! I praise Your glorious Name! You are Creator, Author, Finisher, and the God of mercy. Thank You for loving me, Father. Thank You for never letting go of me. Keep me praising You all day long . Keep me praising You all the days of my life. How I long to worship You in heaven. Until then, help me look to You for everything. Keep my eyes on You, Father, and not on the world. Keep me seeking You and not the worldly things that continue to beckon me. Help me hear Your every whisper and obey Your every command. Fill me with Your Holy Spirit and love so I can love others as You do. Put Your compassion in my heart so I do not miss any opportunity to care for another. Help me bless someone this day. Thank You for hearing my prayer.

Answer: I have an army of angels watching over you, My child.
Response: Thank You, Father, for Your protection and eternal care.

HAVE NO FEAR

O Lord, my God, thank You for showing me that even the great men in the Bible You used for Your great purpose were afraid and felt unworthy. Thank You for each story and each outcome I read about. Thank You for strengthening my faith and speaking to my spirit as I read Your Word. Thank You that I can freely read Your Word and freely worship You. Continue to strengthen me in every way so I may serve You as You have planned. Help me not shy away from Your perfect plan. Ready me for Your service and help me serve with joy. As these days become tedious and the restrictions become more rigid, I pray You lift my spirit to You and allow me to sit in Your presence for a few precious moments. Help me feel the freedom that only You can provide through the gift of Your Son. Thank You for choosing me to know You, Father. Thank You for teaching me and growing me up in You. I ask for more wisdom - as much as You will give me - so I can complete my tasks here on earth as Your servant. Help me bless someone this day. Thank You for hearing my prayer.

Answer: I AM readying you to do My work and am equipping you in every way.

Response: I trust in You, Lord, and pray You calm every fear and lead me in Your work.

DO NOT TARRY!

O Lord, my God, thank You for reminding me You are thinking of me. Thank You for showing me that You have a perfect plan for me. And thank You for being my Help and my Deliverer. There is nothing You won't do for me and nothing You cannot deliver me from. Keep me looking to You as the world turns and churns in chaos. Keep my eyes on You, Lord. May You lead and direct me in the Word so I learn what I need to learn and grow in the spirit. Fill me with Your Holy Spirit so I am led by You, Father. There is a constant struggle between the pull of this world and Your plan for me. Help me hear Your whispers and be obedient to You in all ways. Bend my will to Yours, Lord. Put Your desires in my soul and strengthen me to heed Your will. Pull me to You and show me more of You and Your ways. I ask for more wisdom and I ask for peace. May Your peace be upon me this day and every day. Keep me from evil and from hurting others, Lord. Keep me Yours. Help me bless someone this day. Thank You for hearing my prayer.

Answer: My plans for you are good and not for evil, My child.

Response: Thank You, most gracious and glorious Lord.

HOPE IN GOD

O Lord, my God, thank you for taking care of me and working out every circumstance in my life perfectly. Thank You for showing me I need only wait upon You and You will give me cause to praise You. Help me praise You in the storm. Help me praise You in the many blessings You bestow upon me. Help me praise You in each and every moment of this day. You know what is before me, Father, and I pray You put a song in my heart today. May You fill me with joy as I serve my family. As I look around me and may be burdened with the tasks of this day, help me praise You. Help me find You in every detail of this day. May Your glory shine through. Keep my soul from being disquieted this day. Help me praise You continually even with all I have to do today. Thank You, Lord, for showing me that I can come to You and leave my burdens with You. Thank You for carrying them for me. Help me find rest in You today, Father. Help me bless someone this day. Thank You for hearing my prayer.

Answer: I AM with you, My child, and will put My joy in your heart.

Response: Thank You, Almighty God and Father.

GIFTS WILL BE GIVEN TO YOU

O Lord, my God, thank You for all You have given to me. Thank You for all the blessings You have bestowed upon me. Thank You for all the gifts and talents You have given to me to use for Your purpose. Help me give to others as You have given me. Help me be generous and compassionate and listen to Your gentle whispers as You tell me what to do. Equip and ready me for Your service. Help me do all You have planned for me, Father. Help me seek out those in need and show me where I can serve, Lord. Fill me with Your love so I can fully serve where needed. Help me give freely and serve with joy. Lift my spirit as I give to others. May Your peace cover me this day. Keep my eyes on You, Father. Help me bless someone today. Thank You for hearing my prayer.

Answer: It is My pleasure to bless you, My child, and I will continue to bless you in the days to come.

Response: Thank You, most gracious and loving Father.

YOU HAVE AUTHORITY!

O Lord, my God, thank You for showing me I have authority and power over the enemy. Thank You for giving me both physical and mental strength to overcome this world. And thank You for ensuring that no harm will come to me. I pray You continue to equip me with the strength to overcome all the trials I will face here on earth. May Your peace and rest cover me as I fight the enemies' advances. Lead and guide me in all I do so that I am covered by You, Lord. Fill me with Your Holy Spirit so I remain strong and faithful to You, Father. Help me do all You put me here on earth to do. Help me hear You, Lord, and obey Your commands. Let me not shy away from Your plan. Strengthen me in every way. Help me love as You love and have compassion on those You need to be served. Help me serve with joy and help me bless someone this day. Thank You for hearing my prayer.

Answer: My power and strength are within you, My child, and I am watching over you in all that you do.

Response: Thank You, all powerful and mighty God!

THE SACRIFICE
OF PRAISE

O Lord, my God, thank You for all You do and all You Are. Thank You for creating the universe, the heavens, the earth, and all that is in all of it. Thank You for having me in mind as You created this earth. Thank You for caring for me so perfectly that You placed me here at the perfect time and in the perfect place. Thank You for having a plan and a design for my life. Help me walk into Your plan, Lord. Help me praise You, always, Lord. Keep me in Your Word learning about You and Your Son. Teach me all I need to know. I pray for Wisdom, Lord. I pray You will put wisdom into my heart and soul – as much as You will give me – so I can be perfectly led by You. Forgive my shortcomings and sins, Lord. Keep me from temptation and from evil. Help me not hurt anyone. Help me bless someone today. Thank You for hearing my prayer.

Answer: I AM watching over you and will deliver you from all harm.

Response: Thank You, most gracious God.

THE SACRIFICE
OF PRAISE

O Lord, my God, thank You for the Wisdom in Your Word. Thank You that I can turn to it at any moment and learn about You and be lifted up. Thank You for the blessing of being able to read Your Word and worship You, Lord. Thank You for that freedom today. I pray You continue to watch over our land and continue to bless it. I pray for healing, Lord. May Your healing power go throughout this country and all other countries, Father. May we turn to You and see Your wonder working power. Turn our minds and hearts away from fear and anxiety and help us look to You and worship You. As we worship You, our spirits are lifted. May we praise You as You deserve to be praised! You are Great and Mighty! I praise You, Lord! I love to watch You work. I love to see the miracles that You continue to do in my life, in the lives of my family, and in this world. Help me not miss You, Lord. Help me see all that You are doing so I have even more reason to praise You. Keep my eyes on You, Lord. Help me bless someone this day. Thank You for hearing my prayer.

Answer: I AM working in your life and in your household and will show Myself Mighty and Great in this world.

Response: Thank You, All Powerful and Mighty God.

I HOPE IN YOU

O Lord, my God, thank You for watching over and protecting me. Thank You for working on every circumstance in my life. Thank You for showing me You are ready to help me with all my needs. Thank You for showing me I need only wait on You, hope in You, and expect You to do great things, and You will. You will do Your mighty works as You have in the past. Your plan is far too wonderful for me to understand. Help me believe Your plan is nothing short of miraculous, and then open my eyes so I can fully see You work. Help me trust You in every way, Lord. Even when it doesn't seem like things are going in the right direction, help me know that Your perfect plan is in action. Increase my faith, Lord. Strengthen my spirit so I can withstand all the enemy puts against me. Deliver me from all evil. Keep me from hurting others, Lord. Keep me from sinning against You as I wait upon You. Keep me strong as I wait upon You. Help me be who You desire me to be. Help me bless someone this day. Thank You for hearing my prayer.

Answer: I desire to help you in all ways, My child, and will strengthen you in every way.

Response: Thank You, Almighty and Powerful Lord.

I CALL UPON
THE LORD

O Lord, my God, thank You for showing me You are the God of all and that You watch over me continually. Thank You, Father, for King David's writings that continue to uplift me every time I read his words. As he calls upon You, You hold him up and give him victory, not only in battle but in his everyday life. Thank You, Father, for showing me You desire relationship with me, and that You want to carry my burdens and lift me up and out of my difficulties. You keep me from stumbling around, and if I do stumble, You are there to immediately pick me up. Help me come to You, Father, and give You all that concerns me. May I praise You in the good times and in the storms of life. Help me know You have a plan for the storm and a plan to stop the storm in due time. Your plan is perfect, Lord, and Your will shall be done. Strengthen me in every way and keep my eyes fixed on You. Keep me believing in You and thanking You for every blessing You bestow upon me. Keep me Yours, always. Help me bless someone this day, Father. And thank You for hearing my prayer.

Answer: I AM watching over you and here to pick you up when you fall down, My child.

Response: Thank You, Almighty and Omniscient God and Father.

DO NOT LOSE HEART

O Lord, my God, thank You for reminding me to pray at all times and to continue to pray. Thank You for showing me I am not to be afraid and give up and turn away from Your perfect plan. Thank You for assuring me I should not lose heart but know You will make things come to pass in Your timing. You are God of the Universe and God of my heart. You will do all that I cannot. You lead and guide me through the difficulties of this life and into the blessings You offer. Strengthen me in every way so I can withstand all the trials and remain strong in You, Lord. Keep my eyes on You. Keep my mind on You. Keep me Yours, Lord, no matter what happens to deter me from Your presence. Please keep me Yours. May You lead and guide my every thought, deed, and desire. Make Your desires be my desires, Father. Put Your Holy Spirit in me so I can do as You ask. May Your love flood my soul so I can love others. Help me bless someone this day. Thank You for hearing my prayer.

Answer: I AM with you to strengthen you in every way and hold you up during every trial, My child.

Response: Thank You, Almighty God and Father.

UNTIL CALAMITIES PASS

O Lord, my God, thank You for Your mercy and grace. Thank You for protecting me in the shadow of Your wings. Thank You for helping me see I can be confident in You as I watch the calamity and storm pass along side of me. May You continue to strengthen me when I feel weak. Lift me up when I fall down. Keep me close to You, Father. When the things of this world do not make sense, You do. You care for me in every way. Thank You, most gracious and merciful Father, for working in every circumstance of my life. Help me serve You and give to others amidst the chaos of these days. Show me where I can help, Lord. Open my eyes so that I may see the needs of others and quickly come to their aid. May You shelter me and the family You have given me from this storm, Lord. Help me bless someone this day. Thank You for hearing my prayer.

Answer: I AM with you and your household and will keep you safe.

Response: Thank You, most merciful God and Father.

GOD IS MY DEFENSE

O Lord, my God, thank You for being my Defense. Thank You for being my Fortress. And thank You for being my High Tower. You are my Protector in all ways. Thank You, Father, for watching over me and the family You have given me. Thank You for never leaving us alone. Thank You for Your constant and faithful provision. Increase my faith so I am able to weather every storm and difficulty I will face. Help me wait expectantly upon You for every blessing You have in store for me. You bless me beyond my ability to grasp. Thank You, Lord, for reaching down and saving me. Thank You for Your constant presence. I long for the day when I will kneel before You in heaven. For now, keep me close, Lord. Only You can keep me for I cannot keep myself. Help me draw close to You. Help me bless someone this day. Thank You for hearing my prayer.

Answer: I AM with you, My child, and will keep you as My own for all eternity.

Response: Undeserving of Your grace, thank You, most gracious and merciful Lord.

THE LORD WILL PROVIDE

O Lord, my God, thank You for Your Word that shows me so many tests which have turned into testimonies. Thank You for giving me such beautiful examples to follow as Abraham and his faith. Thank You for showing me I can count on You just as so many others have done. You have blessed the faithful. Help me be faithful to You, Lord. Help me to be obedient to You. Help me hear Your whispers and follow Your commands. Strengthen me in every way and put courage into my soul so I do not fail You, Father. Increase my faith so I do not waiver. As this world is in chaos, help me wait upon You and remain in Your peace. Keep my soul in Your hands and help me to be patient as I wait upon You. May Your peace be upon me and my household. May Your blessings be received, Lord. Help me receive all that You have to give. Help me bless another as You bless me. Thank You for hearing my prayer.

Answer: I AM still the God of Abraham and all those who come to Me, My child, and will strengthen you to live in these days with faith and courage.

POWER BELONGS TO GOD

O Lord, my God, thank You for reminding me that You are All-Powerful and Almighty! Thank You for showing me again and again in Your Word that I can rest in You. I can rest in You when there is chaos all around me. I can depend on You as You work out every detail in my life. There is nothing You do not know or cannot handle for You are the God of the universe. You are the God of my heart and I can depend on You. Help me see You in everything, Lord. Don't let me miss You. Help me see You in the beauty and magnificence of the mountains, the infinite depth of the blue skies, the sun and moon rising each and every day and night. You are wonderful, Lord! You are POWER and MIGHT. I am a speck in the millions of years of our planet, and yet, You know me intimately. You planned my birth and my life. You, and only You, love me more than I can possibly understand. You are my Creator. You are my Hope. You are my Deliverer. Keep my mind on You, today, Father. Show me Your Power as I move through this day. I love to watch You work, Lord. Help me bless someone this day. Thank You for hearing my prayer.

Answer: I AM the Great I AM, and I AM working in your life, My child, and you will always be Mine.

Response: Undeservedly Yours, Lord, thank You for Your grace and mercy.

PRAYING FOR STRENGTH

O Lord, my God, thank You for showing me I need to continually pray for strength to overcome the obstacles of these end days. Thank You for Your Word which breathes life into my spirit. Thank You for sending Your Son to come to this earth to teach us how we should live. Thank You, Father, for every nugget of wisdom You put into my soul. I desire more wisdom, Lord - as much as You will give me. Grant me wisdom and knowledge sufficient to navigate this world at this specific time. Help me hear Your whispers and heed Your commands. May You strengthen me in every way to carry out Your desires, Lord. Help me do all that You have for me to do and grant me the courage to follow You completely. Help me not delay in carrying out Your plan, Father. Keep me at Your feet and seeking Your will for my life. Keep me in constant prayer for strength, Lord. Thank You for watching over me and taking care of all of my needs. Help me bless someone this day. Thank You for hearing my prayer.

Answer: I will strengthen you, My child, so you may withstand all that is before you knowing I AM watching over you.

Response: Thank You, most gracious and powerful God.

JESUS PRAYS FOR US

O Lord, my God, thank You for sending Your Son to come to this earth and willingly give His life for me. Thank You for the gift of salvation. Thank You for the constant intercession of Your Son on my behalf. Thank You for making a way for me to be close to You. Thank You for Your perfect plan to make it possible to see me as perfect even though I am so very flawed. Help me see me as You do, Lord. I praise and worship You, Lord. Sitting in Your presence is the only sacred place for me. You, and You alone, are the lifter of my head. Help me serve You, Father. Show me all You ask me to do and give me the strength to carry out Your plan. Help me bless someone this day. Thank You for hearing my prayer.

Answer: You are Mine, sayeth the Lord.

Response: Undeservedly Yours, Lord.

THE LORD BLESS YOU

O Lord, my God, thank You for all of Your wonderful blessings. Thank You for showing me that You desire to bless all of Your children including me. Help me receive Your blessings and gifts of protection, spiritual enlightenment, grace, mercy, favor, and peace. Keep me from feeling inadequate so I am able to fully receive Your blessings. Forgive me for all my shortcomings and sins and help me receive all You have to offer. Just as You gave these blessings to the Israelites, You desire to give them to me. Thank You, Lord, for Your merciful and loving Spirit. Thank You for all You do and all You are. Fill me with Your Holy Spirit so I can be more like You, Father. May I be more gracious and merciful to others. May I commend others for their good works and show them favor to those around them. May I offer peace to all those who You put me in front of. Help me to bless someone this day. Thank You for hearing my prayer.

Answer: My blessings are for all of My people and for you, My child.

Response: Undeserving of Your blessings, Lord, thank You, most gracious and loving Father.

GRACE THROUGH JESUS

O Lord, my God, thank You for Your perfect plan to save me. Thank You for sending Your Son to sacrifice His life for me and for all people throughout of all the ages. Thank You for making it possible to be in relationship with You. Thank You for choosing me to know You, Lord. Thank You for making me blameless so You can look upon me and see beauty – Your beauty, Lord. You made me as I am and call me to be new in You every day. You give me grace for all my imperfections. You show me how to be better, live better, and give more. You mold me and make me into the person You desire me to be. You ask me to give all I am to You, Lord. Help me continually give my will up to You. Help me desire Your will over mine. This constant battle has raged in me my whole life. Help me finally surrender completely to You, Father. And help me fully worship You, Lord. It is in worshiping You that I lose the cares of this world. Help me truly be Yours, Father. Help me serve You as You desire. Help me bless someone this day. Thank You for hearing my prayer.

Answer: I AM the Great I AM and I desire your worship and your praise.

Response: I praise You, God Almighty, Father of all, and Creator of the universe and all that is in it!

THE WINE WAS
ALL GONE

O Lord, my God, thank You for showing me more about obedience in Your Word and how it leads to miracles. Thank You for showing me how to prepare for a miracle. Lord, I pray You help me be obedient to You in every way. Help me hear Your whispers and carry out Your commands. No matter how insignificant the task seems, help me do what You ask me to do. And then help me see You work. Don't let me miss You working in the circumstances of my life. Thank You for watching over me and taking care of me in every way. Help me look to You to defend me, rescue me, and protect me. Quiet the chaos around me as I rest in You, Lord. May Your will be done, always. Keep me in a constant state of surrender as I give my life and will to You. Sanctify my soul, Lord. Forgive my shortcomings and sins and make me holy in Your sight. Thank You for all You do and all You Are. Help me bless someone this day. Thank You for hearing my prayer.

Answer: I AM with you, My child, to help you do all that I ask.

Response: Help me look to You, Lord, above all else.

NO EYE HAS SEEN

O Lord, my God, thank You for being so present in my life. Thank You for working on my behalf to bring about Your plan for my life. Thank You for working every circumstance out perfectly. Help me continually surrender my life and my will to Yours. Put Your desires in my heart so that I pursue Your will and not my own. Help me do all you ask me to do. I pray for joy in the work that is before me today. Help me attend to all I have to do with joy. May I bring a song of joy to others as well. May we sing Your praises all day long. Help me remember all the mighty works You have done in my life and praise You, Father. You are greatly to be praised! Help me take my eyes off of myself and set my eyes on You. You are Great and Mighty and Grace and Love. You are all good things. As I praise You and wait upon You, You are working on my behalf. May the burdens I carry be lifted today as You take them from me. Thank You, Lord, for being a resting place for my soul. Thank You for taking worry, fear, weakness, and apprehension away from me as You strengthen every part of my being. Thank You, Lord, for allowing me relationship with You, the Great I AM. I am unworthy, Lord, and yet, You count me as worthy. Help me bless someone this day. Thank You for hearing my prayer.

Answer: I AM working on every detail of your life, My child, and will always take care of you.

Response: You amaze me, Lord, that You would count me as Your child and care for me so perfectly.

FATHER, MOLD ME

O Lord, my God, thank You for bringing me close to You. Thank You for choosing me to be Yours. Thank You for continuing to work on me so I can grow into the person You desire me to be. Help me give up my will, continually, and seek Your will. Help me allow You to mold and shape me, Father. May I be easy for You to mold and shape as I let You work on me. Make me Yours, Lord. Please make me Yours. Help me do all You ask me to do. Help me come closer to You so that I can be more like You. Fill me with Your Holy Spirit and lead and guide me in all I do today. May Your grace be upon me as I strive to be more like You. Thank You, Father, for more than sufficient grace. You cover me in every way. Keep me at Your feet, Lord. Help me bless someone this day. Thank You for hearing my prayer.

Answer: I AM working with you, My child, and will continue to mold and shape you as you come unto Me.

Response: Thank You, most gracious and merciful Lord.

BE CONTENT

O Lord, my God, thank You for showing me that Your will is perfect, and You have a plan for each and every one of Your people. Thank You for working out Your plan in my life. Help me fully surrender to You so I can walk into Your plan and leave my plan behind. Help me be obedient to You. Help me be grateful for all You have given to me. Keep me in a place of thankfulness and help me ignore whatever complaints my mind tries to find and think about. Strengthen my soul so I leave worldly desires alone and focus on the wonders of the spirit. Fill me with Your love, Lord, so I may love more deeply and serve more fully. Help me be a true servant of Yours. Help me do for others as You ask of me. Help me serve with joy, Lord. Thank You for giving me the perfect gifts You have given me to do Your will. Lift the burdens I carry and relieve me of the fatigue and pain of this world. May Your peace rest upon me this day as I go about the tasks that I must do. Help me bless someone this day. Thank You for hearing my prayer.

Answer: I have given you many gifts to use to serve My people, and I will help you do as I ask.

Response: Thank You, most gracious and loving Father.

GO IN PEACE

O Lord, my God, thank You for watching over me and the family You have given me. Thank You for being our Great Protector and Defender. Thank You for providing all we need, Lord, and giving us so many things we desire. Thank You for every miracle You have performed before us. Your gifts are bountiful. Your blessings are beautiful. In the quiet, You have shown Yourself to be so merciful, gracious, and loving. Thank You, Lord. Help me always see You work. Don't let me miss any of Your doings in my life. Keep me seeking You over the world, Lord. Keep me at Your feet. May my eyes be raised to the heavens above the pain and struggle of this earth. Help me ponder the wonderful and beautiful, Father. Help me bless others as You bless me, Lord. Help me look for special ways to bless another. Thank You for always hearing my prayer.

Answer: I AM always with you, My child, and take pleasure in watching over, protecting, and blessing you and your household.

Response: Undeserving of Your attention and help, thank You, most gracious and loving Father.

ETERNAL LIFE

O Lord, my God, thank You for being the God of this universe and God of my heart. Thank You for calling me close to You. Thank You for choosing me to know You. Thank You for showing me Who You Are and all You desire to grant me. Thank You for sending Your Son so I have access to You and Your great wonders. Thank You for not withholding anything from me. As I Ask, You grant my requests. As I seek You, I find You and perfect sweetness. I find all things wonderful. Your gift of eternal life and paradise are found here and forever. Help me stay in this perfect precious place of Your presence today, Lord. Lead and guide all that I do. Help me hear Your every whisper and obey Your gentle voice. Help me feel Your love, Father. Thank You for every wonderful generous gift You have given me and desire to give me. May I be Yours forever, Lord. Keep me Yours. Help me bless someone this day. Thank You for hearing my prayer.

Answer: You are My precious child, and You are Mine forever.

Response: Undeservedly Yours, Lord, thank You most gracious and merciful God.

GOD IS PROFOUNDLY IMPRESSIVE

O Lord, my God, You are great and mighty! You are Creator and Maker of all that is. You are peace and love. You are all things wonderful and great. Your ways are too much for me to understand. Your plan is perfect even amongst the chaos of these days. Help me completely rely on You, Lord. Guide me in all that I do. May Your peace reign in this world, Lord. May Your peace reign in my household. Help us look to You for sense out of the senseless. Help us completely rely on You, Father. May You strengthen my household for all the days to come, Lord. Put Your love in our hearts so that we may love fully. Show us the way to You, Father. Keep us under Your care and Your protection. May Your will be done in our land. May Your will be done in our lives. Forgive us all for our sins for we know not what we do. The pain we cause is untold, but You know our hearts. Forgive us, Lord. Thank You, Father, for all You do and all You are. Keep our hearts and eyes on You, Lord, no matter what chaos is looming all around us. Help me bless someone this day. Thank You for hearing my prayer.

Answer: I AM the Great I AM, and I AM working in all things, My child, so rest in Me.

Response: I will rest in You, Father, as I seek Your face.

I WILL HOPE

O Lord, my God, thank You for Your beautiful creation. Thank You for the colors You chose for the grass, trees, skies, mountains, and seas. Thank You for placing me exactly where I am today. Thank You for this beautiful city, state, and country that house so many of Your wonderful creations. Keep me looking to You, Lord. Help me notice You in the wind, the sun, the stillness of the nighttime, the flowers that bloom, and the green grasses that sway to and fro. Help me enjoy the simple, yet glorious, parts of this world that You have made. May Your peace settle over me and the household You have given me. May You fill our hearts with love, Lord. May we keep our eyes fixed on the beautiful and lovely and our hearts stay soft and moldable for You. Lead us and guide us in all we do, Lord. May Your protection be upon us. May You quiet the chaos of this world and touch every heart with Your love and peace. May Your perfect will be done. May no more harm be done. Help me bless someone this day. Thank You for hearing my prayer.

Answer: I AM sending My Holy Spirit to minister to all people who will open their hearts.

Response: May I be open to Your calling, Lord.

PEACE OFFERING

O Lord, my God, thank You for the gift of peace. Thank You for sending Your Son to grant us access to peace. Help me always be thankful as I receive this covering, Lord. At a time when all things seem out of control and distressing, You offer peace. Help me be open to receive peace even in these tumultuous times. Help me know this is a gift that You so generously give to Your people. Help me fully receive what You have to give. Even though I feel unworthy, Your gifts are freely given. Thank You, Lord, for all You do and all You are. Thank You for working in every detail of my life. Help me give the burdens I carry to You. Help me release everything to You so that I may freely give to others, Lord. Ready me for Your service. Help me bless someone this day. Thank You for hearing my prayer.

Answer: My peace is Yours, My child.

Response: Thank You, most gracious and loving God and Father.

HE WILL NEVER REJECT ME

O Lord, my God, thank You for accepting me just as I am. Thank You for Your promise of always accepting me, and never rejecting me. Thank You for choosing me to be Yours. Thank You for showing me more and more of You each day. Thank You for being my calm in the storm. Help me always look to You, Lord, before I look to the world. May Your peace be upon me this day. Help me accept Your love and all You have to give me even when I feel unworthy. Lord, forgive me for all my shortcomings and sins. Help me do better today than yesterday. As I fall short of perfection the shame comes quickly to rob me of Your presence. Bring me back to You as quickly as I fall away. Thank You for the promise of Your love, Father. Although I do not deserve it, You cover me in Your love today and every day. Keep my defenses down so I can allow You to fully love me. Help me stay in Your presence. Help me bless someone this day. Thank You for hearing my prayer.

Answer: You will always be Mine, My child, and I will always love you.

Response: Undeservedly Yours, Lord.

WHERE ARE YOU, GOD?

O Lord, my God, thank You for showing me that You are working even amongst the chaos of our world. Thank You for showing me You are the Most High God now just as You were in the beginning of time and throughout all the ages. Thank You for showing me Your greatness, Lord. Strengthen my faith as I watch so many unsettling things unfold in our country. Grant me wisdom, Lord, to filter out the untruths and find the truth. Keep me seeking You and Your heart when things don't make sense. Let me not turn from You as these days continue. Help me stay inside of Your love so I can love others through the mess and the trouble. Keep my heart soft, Lord. May I serve You and those around me. Help me be joyful in serving. Help me bless someone this day. Thank You for hearing my prayer.

Answer: I AM the Great I AM and I will reign above all as love conquers all.

Response: Keep my eyes on You, Lord, the Great I AM.

WHEN THE EARTH TOTTERS

O Lord, my God, thank You for continually showing me more and more of You. Thank You for leading me to the perfect scripture at the perfect time. The lessons of thousands of years ago are the same lessons we need for today. The experiences of yesteryear help me with today. Today, You are the God Who steadies the pillars of this world. You are the God who holds the world in His hands. You are the God Who is the keeper of my soul and lover of my heart. Thank You, Father, for loving me so perfectly and completely. Thank You for spending time with me when I come to You. Thank You for watching over and protecting me every moment of this day. I take solace in Your presence and care. Help me love others as You love me. Help me see through Your eyes, Lord, and love with Your heart. Help me bless someone this day. Thank You for hearing my prayer.

Answer: I AM with you, My child, and will continue to teach you My ways and show you how to love.

Response: Thank You, most gracious and loving Father.

GOD SHALL BE
WITH THEM

O Lord, my God, thank You for being my Steady during these times of turmoil. Thank You for watching over and protecting me and the family You have given me. Thank You for the promise of a perfect place with You dwelling among Your people. Thank You for the promise of an existence without pain, suffering, tears, and anguish. You are Lord of all. You are Creator of everything. And You desire relationship with me and Your people. May our hearts turn to You, Father. May we come to You with praise and thanksgiving. May we come to You with our needs, pain, suffering, and tears so that You can minister to us. Heal us, Lord. Heal our land. Heal our hearts and heal our minds. Bring us back to You in a powerful way, Father, as we turn to You. May Your hand be upon us and our nation. God bless America. You have blessed us so very much, Lord. May we remain in your care and inside of Your grace. Forgive us our sins and help us look to You to be complete. Thank You for all You do for us and all You are. Help me bless someone this day. Thank You for hearing my prayer.

Answer: I AM with you, your household, and your nation if you will turn to Me, confess your sins, and make Me your God.

Response: Lord, You are the Great I AM, and I will praise You forever. May You grant us all hearts that turn to You.

WALK IN THE LIGHT

O Lord, my God, thank You for sending Your Son to be the Light for me to find in the darkness. Thank You that He continues to lead me into the Life that You have for me. Help me seek You, Lord, and be led and guided by Your Light. As I find You, I can help others find You. Equip me so I can serve others, Lord. Help me do Your will and walk into Your perfect plan. I desire to be used by You. Help me seek You before I seek to satisfy my emotions and desires. May Your desires become mine. As we all find You, Lord, we can be the light for others and light up this world. May we cast Your Light on this planet we call home as we wait to come home to You. Help us worship You, Lord, and give You praise as we long to be in Your presence for eternity. Use us, O God, and keep our hearts soft toward You so that we are obedient to You. Help us bless someone this day. Thank You for hearing our prayer.

Answer: I AM with you and all people who call Me to reside in their hearts and will be the Light as you traverse this world.

Response: Please live in my heart and all who You call to be Yours, Lord.

YOU LED YOUR PEOPLE

O Lord, my God, You are God of this universe and God of my heart. Your wonder working power is shown all throughout the Bible. Your wonder working power is also shown to me and has been shown to me all throughout my life. Thank You for being the God of miracles. Thank You for being the God that sets Your people free. You sent Your Son to live and die so we can live lives abundant in love and peace. Help me live into the freedoms You have given to me so freely. Help me love with the kind of love that changes peoples' lives, Father. Help me grant mercy to those around me. Help me offer grace instead of condemnation. Help me forgive more easily than I feel like forgiving. May Your Holy Spirit flood my spirit today, Father. Lead and guide me through this day. To You be all power and glory, Lord. Help me bless someone this day. Thank you for hearing my prayer.

Answer: I AM the Great I AM and I AM working in all things that are seen and unseen My child, and will fill you with My love.

Response: Thank You, most gracious and powerful God.

IT WAS NOT HIS SIN

O Lord, my God, thank You for showing Yourself miraculous. Thank You for showing me that You are up to miracles in peoples' lives as well as my own. I pray for patience, Lord, while You are working out every circumstance perfectly. Help me wait on You, Father. Increase my faith so I am depending solely on You to solve the complications in my life. Help me hear Your whispers and give me a willing spirit so I carry out Your desires for me. Lead and guide me throughout this day. I only want to follow You. Quiet the chaos around me and grant me Your peace. May Your peace settle over this great nation, Lord. Help us all give our hearts and souls to You, Father. May we come to You for a miracle of miracles. A miracle that will heal our land. Lead us to You, Lord. Soften our hearts and fill us with Your love. May Your Holy Spirit speak to each one of us and keep us calling after You, Lord. Help us each bless someone this day. Thank You for hearing my prayer.

Answer: I AM the God of miracles today just as I WAS thousands of years ago, and I AM watching over you, your household, and your nation.

Response: Turn our hearts to You, Lord.

HOW FORTUNATE ARE WE?

O Lord, my God, thank You for sending Your Son to live and die for me so I could be fully Yours. Thank You for His sacrifice, Father. Thank You that You allowed such an atrocity to happen to Your Son so I could come to You and have relationship with You. Thank You for the ever-flowing grace that is upon me because You can see me, know me, and love me as perfect in Your sight. Thank You for every blessing You bestow upon me, Lord. Thank You for choosing me to be Yours. Thank You for calling me close to You, Father. Thank You for not letting me go and be separate and apart from You. Thank You for the favor You rest upon me every day. And thank You for wanting me to be exclusively Yours. May I worship You all the days of my life. May I sit at Your feet and be filled with Your Holy Spirit. May You soften my heart and bend my will to Yours, Lord. Keep me Yours. Keep me Yours forever. Help me serve You fully and serve Your people. Strengthen me in every way to be of service to You. Help me bless someone this day. Thank You for hearing my prayer.

Answer: My Son saved all people for all time, and I have called you to be Mine, My child, as you will be through all eternity.

Response: Undeserving of Your grace and love, thank You, most gracious God and King.

THE GOOD SHEPHERD

O Lord, my God, thank You for the gift of Your Son Who came to live here on earth. Thank You for Your Word that continues to show me the love You have for me and Your people. Thank You for allowing me to be part of Your flock. Thank You for caring for me in every way. Thank You for allowing me to sit in Your presence as You lead me to pasture and drink of Your living waters. Thank You for feeding and watering my soul. As the world succumbs to chaos, I find You waiting for me to come and be lifted up by Your Holy Spirit. Fill me with Your Spirit as I come to You, Lord, and give me rest. Thank You for Your peace. Thank You for rest and nourishment today and every day. Undeserving of all You give to me, thank You, most gracious and loving Father. Help me serve You as You strengthen me, Lord. I desire to be of service to You and Your people. Help me do all that You have for me to do. Help me bless someone this day. Thank You for hearing my prayer.

Answer: My flock is large, and you are one of My sheep, My child, and I will always take care of you.

Response: Thank You, Almighty God and Father.

THE GOD OF THE UNIVERSE

O Lord, my God, thank You for being the God of this universe. Thank You for Your Might and Power. Thank You for working in every circumstance and situation of our lives and of the lives of all people everywhere. Father, increase our faith and strengthen us to withstand these days and times and remain fully Yours. May Your peace be upon our families, cities, nation, and this world. May we call upon Your Name, Lord. May we come to You and pray more intensely than we have in the past. May we be forever Yours. Help us spread Your love as much and as often as we are able. Show us where You want us to be and whom to give to. Soften our hearts so we are able to be used by You. Help us bless someone this day. Thank You for hearing our prayer.

Answer: I AM at work in your nation, and I am watching over you and your household.

Response: Thank You, Almighty and All-Powerful God.

I NEEDED HOPE TODAY

O Lord, my God, thank You for seeing me. Thank You for seeing the inner most part of my soul. Thank You for filling me with Your Holy Spirit that lights the darkness in me. Thank You for Your Word that assures me You are watching over and protecting me in every way. Thank You for speaking to my heart and lifting me up. May I sit in Your presence for a few precious moments this day and be filled with Your love. Strengthen me, Lord, as I feel weak. Your power floods my soul and gives me strength to love others and be kind in the midst of pain. Help me do Your will, Lord. May I follow You above all else. Help me seek Your peace amongst the chaos of this world. Help me hear Your voice above the noise around me. Keep me in Your care, Father. Help me bless someone this day. Thank You for hearing my prayer.

Answer: I AM with you, My child, and I see your needs.

Response: Thank You, most gracious and loving Father.

GOD HAS A PLAN

O Lord, my God, thank You for showing me You have a plan today just as You had a plan two thousand years ago. Thank You for showing me You will not leave me abandoned, but You have a plan to work out all things for Your glory. Help me be obedient to You in all things. Help me hear Your whispers and obey Your commands. Keep my heart seeking after You, Lord. May You strengthen me in every way to withstand all advances of the enemy. Keep me from temptation, Father, and keep me from hurting others. Show me where I can be of service to another and lift up instead of tear down. Help me be a beacon of light that leads back to You, Lord. May Your will be done in my life and in all the lives of people everywhere. Help us all draw close to You and heed Your call, Father. May we follow You and help carry out Your plan. Help me bless someone this day. Thank You for hearing my prayer.

Answer: I AM working in every circumstance and My plan will be done.

Response: Help me serve You in all things, Lord.

GLADNESS AND SIMPLICITY

O Lord, my God, thank You for Your Word. Thank You for filling my spirit today with Your Word. Thank You for encouraging me as I desperately needed to be. Thank You for brighter days to come which will be filled with more with gladness, simplicity, and generosity. Help me stand and face today with strength and love as You assure me there are better days to come. Fill my heart with love so I may give Your love to others even as division and pain seem to overcome our nation. Your love is able to cover the atrocities and abominations that are taking place. Your love can light the path, Father. Lead us and guide us with Your Light. Help us follow You, Lord, as we go about our days. Continue to encourage our hearts so we may be a beacon for someone that crosses our path. Bring us all to You, Lord. May our knees bow down to You, Father. Help me bless someone this day. Thank You for hearing my prayer.

Answer: I AM watching over you and the nation, My child, and will bring gladness, simplicity, and generosity to you all.

Response: I look forward to simpler days, Lord. Thank You for Your Word that encourages me today.

I'M NOT LAUGHING

O Lord, my God, thank You for showing me, once again, there is nothing too hard or too wonderful for You to do or accomplish. Thank You for showing me You have a perfect plan for each and every one of us. Thank You for showing me that You do not go back on Your Word. From the beginning of time Your Word spoke into existence this world and created each of us. Help us all turn to You in our time of need. Help us know You will lead us into victory. Your plan is for Your glory and may not look like what we have asked for, but You answer our prayers perfectly. Give us patience to wait on You. Strengthen us to stand in the midst of the storm. Keep our eyes on You, Lord, and keep us looking to the heavens for our rescue. Soften our hearts and fill us with Your love. Help us cling to Your promises and not laugh at Your plan for us. Help us bless someone this day. Thank You for hearing our prayer.

Answer: I AM working in your life and all the lives of My people. Hold fast to my Word for it will come to pass.

Response: Strengthen us, Lord, to stay strong during this time of unrest and fill us with Your love.

LOVE ONE ANOTHER

O Lord, my God, thank You for Your love. Thank You for sending Your Son so that I may be filled with Your Holy Spirit and be guided by You. Help me love those around me today, Father. Help me love Your People. I pray for all those who don't know You yet. May they come to know You and love You as their Lord and Savior. May Your wisdom flood my soul so I act as You would have me act. Help me see through Your eyes, Lord. Help me do all You have for me to do. Give me courage to stand on Your Word. Strengthen me in every way so that I may be used by You. Set a guard upon my mouth so I do not use my words to tear down. Help me build up another today, Lord. May Your Holy Spirit pour into my soul today. Lead and guide all that I do, Lord. May my thoughts turn to You throughout this day. Help me consider all the wonderful things You have done and set my heart on those things, Lord. Help me love as You love. Help me bless someone this day. Thank You for hearing my prayer.

Answer: I AM love and desire love for all My people.

Response: Help me love as You do, Lord.

MY FATHER'S HOUSE

O Lord, my God, thank you for encouraging me today. Thank You for preparing a place for me to reside with You for all eternity. Thank You for the promise of coming back for me. Thank You for the promise of Your eternal presence with me. Help me live out the rest of my days according to Your will and plan for my life. Help me do all the things You have for me to do. I desire to be used by You, Lord. I want to help bring people to You to experience Your glory. Lead and guide me as I wander this earth, Father. May I sit in Your presence for a few precious minutes as the world spins seemingly out of control. May Your peace be upon me. Help me see You in the beauty that surrounds me. Help me see You in the moments of today. Help me bless someone this day. Thank You for hearing my prayer.

Answer: I AM with you here on earth, My child, and will be with you for eternity.

Response: Thank You, most gracious and loving Father.

DO NOT LET.....

O Lord, my God, thank You for showing me Your Power in Your Word today. Thank You for showing me I am not to allow my heart to be troubled. Thank You for showing me that I am commanded to believe in You and believe in Your Son. And that I am not to let my feelings destroy the magnificence of You – the sacrifice Your Son made in order for me to have victory. Strengthen me in every way so I can fully trust in and rely on You. You are Creator of all I see, Lord, and You will reign! Your plan is for Your glory! Help me serve You and be used to further Your plan, Lord. I pray You will strengthen all of Your people to stand strong and be filled with Your Light. Lead and guide us so we may lead and guide others to You, Father. Light the path and give us courage to walk it. May Your Holy Spirit sweep through our spirits and lift us up so we can lift up others. Help us bless someone this day. Thank You for hearing our prayer.

Answer: I AM to be trusted in every way and will strengthen you so you will not let distress take over your heart and mind.
Response: Thank You, Father, for strengthening me and granting me peace.

PEACE IS A GIFT

O Lord, my God, thank You for Your covering of peace. Thank You for giving us Your peace. Thank You for showing me I need to set aside other emotions like fear and agitation to be able to receive Your peace. Help me set my mind on You so I do not let other emotions flood my soul. Keep me Yours, Lord. While chaos ensues around me, help me press in and seek You. May Your Holy Spirit fill my soul and flood my mind. Help me remember all the wonderful things You have done for me to keep me safe and bring me closer to You, Father. I praise Your Name! You are greatly to be praised! You have come to my aid in every situation, Lord. You have rescued me time and time again. And You will continue to be My Rescuer. Lead and guide me this day. Help me bless someone today. Thank You for hearing my prayer.

Answer: My peace I grant to you, My child, and you will remain in it.

Response: Thank You, most gracious and merciful Father.

DO NOT FALTER

O Lord, my God, thank You for Your Word. Thank You for Jesus' words that bring clarity and wisdom to my mind and soul. Strengthen me, Lord, so I do not falter or fall away. Help me do all I can do to be strong and not waiver in my mind. Strengthen me to face everything I will face and remain steadfast to You. May Your peace be upon me and my household. May You watch over and protect us. Lead and guide us in all that we do. Keep us in Your care, Father. Keep us Yours. As You strengthen us, may we go out and help others. Help me bless someone this day. Thank You for hearing my prayer.

Answer: You and your household are Mine, sayeth the Lord.

Response: Undeservedly Yours, Lord, thank You.

THE CLOUD

O Lord, my God, thank You for leading and guiding me. Thank You for the trials that come my way which help me learn to lean on You. Thank You for helping me develop obedience to You and increase my faith in You. Through every trial and difficulty, I have learned to rely on You more. I have learned to trust You. I pray for more faith and more obedience. Increase my faith, Lord. Help me hear Your whispers and obey You. Strengthen me so I can be used by You. Ready me for Your service. Mold me and shape me as You guide me through this life. Help me be flexible to Your calling. Thank You for choosing me to know You and calling me close to You. Help me bless someone this day. Thank You for hearing my prayer.

Answer: I AM leading and guiding you, My child, and will continue to grow your faith in Me so that you are obedient to My calling.

Response: Thank You, most gracious and loving Father.

TAKE COURAGE

O Lord, my God, thank You for working out every circumstance in my life. Thank You for Your Word that strengthens me, gives me courage, and reminds me You already have won. You are the Victor. You have overcome the world. May Your perfect peace be mine. May You wrap Your peace around me like a blanket that cannot come undone. Help me put every ounce of faith I have been given in You, Lord. Put Your praise in my heart. I praise You, Lord. I praise Your Holy Name! You are greatly to be praised! Keep me close to You, Father. Keep me at Your feet during every trial and difficulty. Keep me looking to You. Help me bless someone this day. Thank You for hearing my prayer.

Answer: I AM the Great I AM and there is nothing that I will not do for you, My child.

Response: You are Great and are greatly to be praised!

A LOVE SO GREAT

O Lord, my God, thank You for sending Your Son here to be the Lamb that saved the world. Thank You for allowing Him to leave Your side to live as a man with all the pain that is here on earth. Thank You, Jesus, for leaving heaven's door to come to us and give Yourself to save us. Thank You for loving each and every one of us so deeply that Your mission to save us came before You saving Your own life. Continue to teach me and help me give freely of myself. Help me serve with a true servant's heart. Help me give beyond what I think is possible, Lord. Keep my eyes on You as I serve others. Help me love as You love. Help me live with eternal life here and now. Help me grow and be all You desire me to be and do all You have for me to do. Strengthen me and give me courage to be wholly obedient to You, Father. Help me bless someone this day. Thank You for hearing my prayer.

Answer: My plans for you are wonderful, My child, and I will equip you to do all I have planned for you.

Response: Undeserving of Your love and attention, thank You, most gracious and loving Father.

KEEP AND PROTECT THEM

O Lord, my God, thank You for Your Son Who not only gave His life for me, but He continues to pray for me. Thank You for His heart that holds all Your people in His prayers to You. May You, indeed, sanctify me – make me holy. Keep me in Your Word, Lord, so I can learn more Truth. Keep me seeking You. Help me be strong enough to walk in Truth as calamity and chaos continue to swirl around me. May Your whispers flood my soul. May Your Holy Spirit fill me so I can be more like You – love like You - love and bless others as You bless me. Keep my heart soft toward You, Lord. Keep me at Your feet. Keep me Yours forever. May I rest in Your presence for a few precious moments today. May I rejoice in You, Lord. You are greatly to be praised! Help me bless someone this day. Thank You for hearing my prayer.

Answer: You are Mine forever, My child.

Response: Undeservedly Yours, Lord, thank You.

GRACE AND FAVOR

O Lord, my God, thank You for the promises in Your Word. Thank You for the promise of guidance and lighting the path I walk. Thank You for being my Protector in all things. Thank You for the unearned grace and favor You so lovingly shower over me. Thank You for every blessing You have already blessed me with and all the blessings You have in store for me. Thank You for lifting me up this morning and giving me hope. Help me walk into the glory You have planned. Help me serve You with all my heart as I walk this earth. As I face every trial, help me remember You will turn every adversity into a praise as I keep my eyes on You. Fill me with Your love, Lord, Keep me close to You. Help me bless someone this day. Thank You for hearing my prayer.

Answer: I AM with you, My child, and will guide you and protect you from all harm.

Response: Thank You, Almighty God and Father.

THE PEOPLE GRUMBLED

O Lord, my God, thank You for all You do for me and all You are. Thank You for blessing me so undeservedly with all I need and so many of the things I desire. Thank You for showing me the path ahead and giving me the strength and persistence to keep moving forward. Thank You for bringing me the perfect thing at the perfect time. Thank You for working in every circumstance of my life. May I look to You and praise Your Name! Put Your praise in my heart, Father. Help me praise You day and night. You are worthy to be praised! I worship You, Lord. You are wonderful, awesome, and all that I need. Keep me focused on You, Lord. Keep my eyes on You. Fill me with Your Holy Spirit and help me walk in Your love. Forgive me for complaining, Lord, and replace that with gratefulness. Help me bless someone this day. Thank You for hearing my prayer.

Answer: I AM working out My perfect plan for your life, My child.

Response: Thank You, Almighty and All-Powerful God.

GOD'S POWER

O Lord, my God, thank You for the perfect Word today. Thank You for showing me You are God Almighty, and I am safe with You. Thank You for watching out for me and protecting me and the family You have given me. Thank You for caring for us in every way. Thank You for providing all we need, Lord. Thank You for all the big and small ways I see You working in our lives. May Your watch and protection over us continue. May You keep us as Yours, Lord. Help us walk in truth as we navigate this world. Help us spread Your love and build bridges of hope. Strengthen us in every way so we may be used by You, Father. Thank You for all You do and all You are. Thank You for Your peace and assurance that You are God of all and that Your will is done. Help us walk into Your perfect plan. Help me bless someone this day. Thank You for hearing my prayer.

Answer: I AM with you and your household, My child, and will care for you in every way.

Response: Thank You, most gracious and loving Father.

THE TRUE SCOPE
OF LIFE

O Lord, my God, thank You for sending Your Son to this earth to teach me about You. Thank You for all the Wisdom in Your Word. Thank You for saving me from my sins and for showing me the true meaning of life which is knowing You. Thank You for making Yourself available to me. I am transformed by Your Holy Spirit. You continue to change me so I can love more fully and give more completely. Help me serve You, Father. Help me do all You have for me to do. Keep my heart seeking You, Lord. Increase my faith in You. I pray for Wisdom, Lord, as much as You will give me so I can do Your will. Fix all of me that is broken so I can serve You better. May Your will be done in my life and the lives of Your people. All glory and power is Yours, Lord. Help me bless someone this day. Thank You for hearing my prayer.

Answer: I AM giving you all you need so you can do My will, My child.

Response: Thank You, Almighty God and Father.

PERMIT IT

O Lord, my God, thank You for showing me I need to follow Your leading and guiding because it is right, correct, and perfect. Help me follow You no matter what the circumstances. Help me be wholly obedient to You, Father. Help me not question You or waiver in carrying out Your instructions. Keep me close to You and fully strengthened by Your Holy Spirit. Ready me for Your service in every way. Help me bend to Your will, Father. Help me do all You ask me to do. Keep my spirit completely aligned with Yours. Consume my soul, Lord, as I commune with You. Help me bless someone this day. Thank You for hearing my prayer.

Answer: I AM with you and am preparing you to do My work, My child.

Response: Strengthen me in every way, Lord.

GOD WILL DELIVER US

O Lord, my God, thank You for strengthening me through Your Word. Thank You for reminding me You are merciful, loving, and kind. Thank You for reminding me that I can trust in You and rely on You. Thank You for reminding me You will never forsake me. Help me find You in this storm, Lord. Strengthen me and then light the path for me, Almighty God. Lead and guide me this day. Help me be obedient to You and only listen to Your voice. Keep me Yours, Lord. As I falter and weaken, keep me Yours. Increase my faith as I walk through this day. Help me praise Your beauty at the start of this day. You are greatly to be praised! Help me bless someone today. Thank You for hearing my prayer.

Answer: I AM all you need, My child, and will strengthen you as you have need.

Response: Thank You, Almighty and All-Powerful God.

ANXIETY AND WORRY

O Lord, my God, thank You for leading me back to peace. Thank You for assuring me that You will take care of me in all situations and circumstances as I seek You. Thank You for Your perfect peace. Thank You for sending Your Son to give His life so I can sit in Your presence and be filled with Your Holy Spirit. Help me seek You over the world. Increase my faith as these uncertain times continue. Strengthen my spirit as the uncertainty becomes more real every day. Keep my eyes on You and help me bend my will to Yours. Help me be obedient to Your whispers and hold fast to Your Word. Lead and guide me this day, Father. May Your peace wrap around me like a blanket as I know You are caring for me in every way. Help me bless someone this day. Thank You for hearing my prayer.

Answer: I AM watching over you, My child, and My peace is upon you.

Response: Thank You, most gracious and merciful Lord.

MY PERSONAL BRAVERY

O Lord, my God, thank You for being my Strength. Thank You for Your perfect plan that is far beyond my comprehension. Thank You for showing me Your plan is still the plan for all time and You are working out everything perfectly according to Your glory. Thank You for helping me grow during the difficulties and trials that are upon me. Thank You for helping me move through them as You are my guide, my strength, and my courage. Help me learn all I need to learn to move forward spiritually, Lord. Please help me dig in and do all You desire for me to do. Don't let me back down in fear. Instill in me a greater faith in You, Lord. Lift me up when I fall down and sturdy my steps as I walk into the unknown. Thank You for being my All in All. Thank You for never leaving me abandoned. Thank You for assuring me You are the God of the universe and the God of my heart. May I bend to You, always. Help me bless someone this day. Thank You for hearing my prayer.

Answer: I AM the Great I AM and My will shall be done.

Response: Help me do Your will, Almighty God and Father.

SERVING

O Lord, my God, thank You for showing me that serving others is of primary importance in Your kingdom. Thank You for gently enfolding me in Your love as You show me more about how to live inside of Your will. As You lead and guide me Your mercy is upon me. I can feel Your grace wash over me as You show me more about how to live and be closer to You as I do Your will. Strengthen me as I move through this day. I pray You will put joy in my heart and soul as I serve others, Lord. I pray for a joyful heart. Help me do as You ask and follow Your gentle whispers. Help me bless someone this day. Thank You for hearing my prayer.

Answer: I AM asking you to serve My people and I will give you the strength to do so and will bless you as you follow Me.

Response: Thank You, most merciful and gracious God.

THE ELEVENTH HOUR

O Lord, my God, thank You for being the God of miracles. Thank You for working out every circumstance in my life. Thank You for coming to me in the eleventh hour so I can see You work as the Almighty God that You are. Thank You for all You do for me and All You are. You are the God of the universe and God of my heart. I pray You will continue to increase my faith through every trial I go through and every miracle I see You do. Help me see You work, Lord. I do not want to miss You. I praise You, Father! I praise Your holy name! Help me look to You for help and assurance instead of the world. Keep my eyes on You, Lord. May my heart and soul be filled with Your love and wisdom. Help me bless someone this day. Thank You for hearing my prayer.

Answer: I AM the God Who sees your need, My child, and I will take care of you.

Response: Thank you, Almighty and All-Powerful Lord.

BLESSED QUIET
FOR YOUR SOUL

O Lord, my God, thank You for replacing my burdens, trials, and worries with Your peace, rest, and blessed quiet. Thank You for quieting my soul as it spins out of control with the worries of this day and the days ahead. Help me stay in a place of peace, Lord. Keep the burdens from overtaking my mind and the chaos from ruling my life. I desire peace. I desire rest. Your Word says that as I learn of You and take Your yoke upon me I will find quiet for my soul. Thank You, Lord, for this gift. Help me receive it wholly and completely. Help me rest in You and stay in Your peace. Help me not take back the burdens I place at Your feet. Keep my eyes on You as I move through this day. Lead and guide me in all I do and keep my heart at peace. Help me serve with joy and give to those around me, Father. Help me do all You have for me to do today and do the best that I can do in service to You. Strengthen me in every way, Lord, so I do not waiver. Help me bless someone this day. Thank You for hearing my prayer.

Answer: My peace is yours, My child, and I will ease your burdens.

Response: Thank You, most gracious and merciful Lord.

MERCY

O Lord, my God, Your Word says I should offer mercy. Jesus told the Pharisees that mercy is preferred over sacrifice. Help me generously and freely offer mercy to others just as Jesus died to offer me mercy. Help me be ready to help those around me without hesitation. Help me spare others and prefer them over my own needs. Help me offer forgiveness freely and generously, Lord. Find any weakness or hardness in my heart and soul, Father, and mend it so I may be a servant of mercy. Thank You for sending Your Son so I may be freely forgiven and have a relationship with You. Thank You for loving me so much that You were able to offer up Your Son as a sacrifice for all people everywhere from the beginning of time to the end of time. May we, as a people, forgive all those around us, Father, and become Your servants of mercy. Help me bless someone this day. Thank You for hearing my prayer.

Answer: I desire mercy, My child, and not rules and religion from My people.

Response: Soften my heart, Lord, so I may be a servant of mercy.

FINDING SHELTER

O Lord, my God, thank You for the constant shelter You provide for me – shelter from the storms of life and sweet calm for my soul. Thank You for sending Your Son to us to teach us and sacrifice His life for us so we may partake of Your Kingdom here on earth. You sweeten my soul. You heal my body and heart. You are a constant place of shelter for me, Lord, and I thank You. Help me accept the sweet gifts You give to me and find continued rest even amongst the chaos. Help me serve those around me with joy, Father. Help me do as You ask me to do without complaint. Infuse my soul with Your Holy Spirit so I can help others beyond my human ability, Lord. I desire to be of service to You. Thank You for choosing me to know You and worship You. Help me bless someone this day. Thank You for hearing my prayer.

Answer: I AM with you, My child, to help you do My work and give you rest as you have need.

Response: Thank You, most gracious and merciful Lord.

A JOYFUL NOISE

O Lord, my God, thank You for Your Word. Thank You for the joy Your Word instills in my heart. Thank You for opening my heart and soul to You as I read it. I praise You, Father! I praise You because You, alone, are Holy. I Praise You because You are Creator of all good and wonderful things. I praise You because You chose me to know You. I praise You because You made a way for me to know You and a way to worship You. I praise You for Your Son's sacrifice. You graciously gave Your Son to us so we could come to know You better. He taught us with every word He spoke. His words are Wisdom and were instilled in His heart by You, Almighty God. Thank You for such a sacrifice, Lord. Thank You for every detail You worked out in the past, present, and will work out in the future. Your plan is perfect and will be done. Help me walk into Your perfect will, Lord. I desire to be of service to You, the Great I AM. Help me bless someone this day. Thank You for hearing my prayer.

Answer: I AM the Great I AM and My will shall be done, My child.
Response: Help me be obedient to Your call, Father.

THE BATTLE IS
THE LORD'S

O Lord, my God, thank You for taking the battle away from me. Thank You for already knowing the outcome and working everything out for Your glory and my good. Thank You for taking care of me in every way. Help me remember all that You have done for me and all the promises that are yet to come. Increase my faith and strengthen my belief in You, Lord, as these days continue to pass with still new issues to fear. May You equip me with courage as I move through this day and all future days. Although it seems the chaos is worsening, help me know it is all a part of Your plan. Your plan is perfect, Lord, and I have no cause to question You. Strengthen me in every way so I can be of service to You. Help me do all You have planned for me to do. Help me bless someone this day. Thank You for hearing my prayer.

Answer: I have already won every battle you will face, My child, and will strengthen you to walk through each one in victory.

Response: Thank You, Almighty and All-Powerful Lord and God.

THOUGHTS ARE POWERFUL

O Lord, my God, thank You for showing me about the thoughts we think. Thank You for showing me that my thoughts have an impact on others and the way they perceive me. Help me see me as You do so I can think better of myself. Help me see the beauty You created and the strength You have infused in me. Keep me from lessening Your perfect plan for me, Lord. Keep me from thinking and saying destructive things about myself. Increase my faith so I am able to walk into the promised land You have prepared for me. Help me receive all the blessings You still have in store for me. Keep me from destroying Your perfect plan for me. Keep my thoughts on You and Your strength, protection, and care for me. Help me bless someone this day. Thank You for hearing my prayer.

Answer: I AM working beside you, My child, to bring you into victory.

Response: Help me do all that You desire for me to do, Lord.

HE WHO WALKS ON THE WIND

O Lord, my God, thank You for Your beautiful creation. Thank You for making the heavens and the universe for us to gaze upon in wonder. You are magnificent and majestic in every way. We cannot possibly mimic Your beauty, Father. Help us see You everywhere. Help us not miss You, Lord. May joy and thankfulness rise up inside us as we look upon Your creation. May we know and understand that You work in every detail of our lives just as You tend to every detail of every flower, tree, and bird. You care about each of us in a truly significant way and have our lives planned out perfectly. Help us rest in You today knowing that Your perfect plan is in place. May Your peace be upon this day as we seek You in all we see and do today. Help us bless someone this day. Thank You for hearing our prayer.

Answer: I AM the Great I AM and I have made all things beautiful.

Response: I praise Your Name, Lord, and thank You for the beauty that surrounds me.

THEIR ANGELS LOOK UPON THE FACE OF GOD

O Lord, my God, thank You for showing me how much You truly care for me and the children You have given me. Thank You for Your Word that says their angels are constantly in Your presence and looking upon You, the Creator of this universe. Thank You, Father, for Your reassurance the current uncomfortable situations we are all experiencing are still under Your control. Help me seek You more earnestly. Keep me Yours, Father, through this storm and all storms of this life. Keep my eyes on You. Help me turn off the noise filled with chaos and listen to You and Your gentle whispers. May the world's hearts turn to You, Lord. May we give You all our concerns and worries in exchange for Your peace. May Your peace descend upon us as a warm blanket on a cool winter evening. May Your comfort rest inside of our souls. May Your love permeate our hearts, Lord. Help us bless one another during these days of unrest. Thank You for hearing our prayers, Father.

Answer: I AM still speaking to My people and will give My peace and rest to all who call upon My name.

Response: Thank You, most gracious and loving Father.

I AM IN THE MIDST OF THEM

O Lord, my God, thank You for Your Word once again that encourages and uplifts my spirit. Thank You for Your promises. Thank You for being so alive among Your people. No matter if it is just two that gather You are in the midst of them. Thank You for showing me Your grace, Lord. Thank You for the special things You do for me that only I can see. Thank You for constantly speaking to and filling my Spirit with You. Keep me seeking You, Lord. Keep me at Your feet. Keep me Yours through these trials and unto eternity. May I be forever Yours. Strengthen me so I do not turn away from You during the difficulties of today and future days. Help me hold fast to You and Your Word. Ready me for Your service. Help me serve You in a way that will glorify Your Name. You are greatly to be praised, Father! I praise Your Name! Help me bless someone this day. Thank You for hearing my prayer.

Answer: I AM with you, My child, and will strengthen you so you can serve My people.

Response: I wait upon You, Lord.

THE LORD NEEDS IT

O Lord, my God, thank You for teaching me to listen. Thank You for slowing me down inside of the seemingly endless duties I have so I can take time and listen to You. Help me obey Your every command. Help me see I am blessed beyond measure when I listen to You and obey. May Your will be done over mine. Help me set aside my desire to accomplish the things that are in front of me to take the precious time with my family that will never be recaptured once gone. May Your grace be upon me so all the little things can be easily done in order to attend to the greater things today. Help me be present in every moment with my family. Help me set aside any resentment I have about serving and help me serve with joy. May I hear every whisper, Lord. May you show me the beauty that every moment of this day provides. Don't let me miss You, Lord. Don't let me miss You and Your perfect plan. May Your peace settle upon me and my mind. May Your peace be upon this household. Help me bless someone today, Lord. Thank You for hearing my prayer.

Answer: I AM with you and will bless these precious moments with your family at your side.

Response: Thank You, most gracious and blessed Lord.

OPEN BOOK TEST

O Lord, my God, thank You for Your Word. Thank You for the promises of Your Word. Thank You for the encouragement and strength I find as I read Your Word. Help me continue to seek You as these difficult times press upon me. Help me remember the miracles You have already done for me and be reminded of Your goodness and blessings upon my life. Help me believe in the promises of Your Word. Increase my faith as I move through the obstacles of this day. Put joy in my heart as I serve those around me. With all my being I desire to serve You. Prepare me for today and the days ahead. May I sit in Your presence for a few precious moments and be strengthen by You. Your grace and mercy flow generously over my soul. Thank You, Father, for always taking care of me in the most perfect way. Help me bless someone this day. Thank You for hearing my prayer.

Answer: I AM with you, My child, and My promises are true for you and all those who believe in and rely on Me.

Response: Thank You, Almighty and All-Powerful Lord and God.

ACKNOWLEDGMENT

I would like to thank Tracy A. Brennan for being a champion cheerleader. She has so generously given her time and expertise in editing this book. She is an amazing human-being and her talents are innumberable! Thank you, Tracy, for your friendship and your assistance in more ways than I can count!

Thank you to pixabay photographer, design. meliora, for the picture used for the book cover.

I thank the Lord for continuing to lead and guide me, hear me as I write to Him, answer back, and propel me to share with others. He is my Beacon as I wade through the waters of life.

ABOUT THE AUTHOR

Andrea Lende

Andrea Lende writes daily devotions and prayers which instill hope, gratefulness, and strength to her readers. She shares her messages through her online ministry at www.believinghim.com and hosts a daily podcast, Downloads from God.

BOOKS BY THIS AUTHOR

God Is Still Almighty

Is God still in control? These are questions so many are grappling with in our world today. You can maintain peace and joy and grow in faith during these difficult times. God is Still ALMIGHTY will inspire you to see God's protection, provision, and His care for you in your everyday life. As you read each day's devotion and prayer your hope in Christ will come to life. God's comfort and mercy will wash over you as you read the words inspired by Him. His love will fill your spirit and your relationship will deepen as you see Him work in your life.

Life After Lupus

Andrea was diagnosed with lupus, an autoimmune disease, when she was thirty years old. It took her three years to regain her health, which she did through diet and natural remedies. She shares her inspirational journey to help others live a life of healing, love, and thankfulness. Andrea has authored three additional books, writes and publishes daily prayers and meditations, and has written over one hundred songs. She speaks to many about her recovery.

A Mother's Love

This book is a compilation of poetry and prayers written for my children as they transitioned into young adulthood. My innermost thoughts as a mother, which are universal to all mothers, are written in these pieces. They encapsulate my son's younger selves and their adult selves and are my true wishes for their best selves. My prayer is the Lord will enfold them in His love as they journey through this life. These writings will bless every mother in every season of motherhood. They will tug at all the heart strings we, as mothers, experience while sharing wisdom with both young and seasoned moms. One of the most difficult things to do as a mother is to learn to let go as our babies become toddlers who then become children, teenagers, and finally, young adults. These pieces will help lessen the pain of letting go and instill gratefulness during the journey. Several of the writings are prayers for my children. These prayers will bless all mothers who need prayer for themselves and their children.

God's Whispers And Melodies

Transformation is experienced differently for every person. Andrea Lende writes about how the Lord transformed her heart through the music and lyrics God gave her. She allows herself to be vulnerable as she shares the Kingdom lessons she was taught with each new song she wrote. Andrea thought God was calling her to a music ministry, when He was actually using the music to connect with her spirit in a way she could understand. Her journey through music and lyrics will undoubtedly connect with your spirit and inspire a closer walk with the Lord.

Made in United States
North Haven, CT
08 January 2022

14349279R00064